Surviving
Point Blanche Prison

A twisted tale of true events by

Alesco E. Violenes

Surviving Point Blanche Prison

Publisher:
Alesco E. Violenes

Alescoviolenes@gmail.com

ISBN: 9798878228169

Table of Contents

Overview

I was born, raised, and imprisoned on an island paradise. This memoir chronicles my 19-year journey through Point Blanche Prison in Sint Maarten and what led me there.

Following a Hurricane, my family relocation where challenging dynamic financial struggles, overcrowding, and my stepfather's alcoholism—pushed me toward street life as I tried to provide for myself and my siblings.

Rather than glorifying crime, I present it as a consequence of the environment and limited choices. The narrative shifts from incarceration to transformation, exploring how prison became an unexpected catalyst for personal growth through music, education, and mentorship.

The book concludes with reflections on reintegration and my commitment to helping others avoid similar paths, offering insight into rehabilitation and redemption without romanticizing the difficult journey.

A Tapestry of Early Years

My journey began in the vibrant landscapes of Sint Maarten, where the echoes of my early years are etched in the corners of Middle Region, now known as GV.

The canvas of my memories paints a picture of a time when I, a wide-eyed child, shared a home with my mother and grandfather in the early '90s.

While the details blur, the silhouette of my grandfather stands vividly in my recollections.

However, the tranquility of those days was shattered when he peacefully departed in his sleep, leaving a profound impact on my nascent understanding of life.

At that juncture, I stood as the sole offspring of my mother and father, with the anticipation of a new sibling lingering, yet unborn.

The turning tide of 1997 ushered in a relocation to Dutch Quarter, a neighborhood stamped with the character of Union Farm, later metamorphosing into the government emergency homes, now aptly named the 911 Projects.

For a child, residing in the projects held its own set of experiences. Dutch Quarter, draped in a reputation of ruggedness and marred by crime, demanded resilience even from the young.

As the environment whispered tales of its unforgiving nature, the seed of toughness was sown in the heart of a child.

The need to carve a name for oneself became an unwritten rule, a passport to recognition and belonging in the tapestry of Dutch Quarter life.

Yet, amidst the challenges, a poignant moment stood frozen in time - the passing of my grandfather.

While still in the tender age of four, the shadows of his departure cast ripples that would reverberate through the years to come.

I stood witness to the birth of my second brother, an event overshadowed by the bittersweet symphony of life's inevitable cycles.

The Unforgiving Streets: A Necessity Born of Struggle

As the chapters of my life unfolded, the challenges within our family deepened, and the narrative of my existence became entwined with the complex dynamics of Dutch Quarter.

The landscape painted itself with hues of adversity and resilience, setting the stage for a trajectory that would defy conventional norms.

In the backdrop of Union Farm, the relationship with my stepfather transformed into a tempestuous journey. The weight of emotional strife intensified, casting shadows on the sanctuary that a home should be.

Cruelty, a bitter companion, found its place, disproportionately directed towards my second brother and me.

The warmth of familial bonds frayed at the edges, leaving me to grapple with the unsettling reality of being an outsider within the walls of my own home.
A necessity emerged from the chaos - an escape to the streets, not just to evade the turmoil but to shoulder the responsibility of providing for my siblings.

The financial strains, coupled with the erratic behavior of my stepfather, compelled me to embrace a role that transcended my age.

The streets, with their alluring promises of quick gains and a semblance of control, beckoned as a refuge, and I embarked on a journey that would redefine my understanding of survival.

A Complex Weave: Threads of Resilience and Adversity

In the intricate tapestry of my existence, Dutch Quarter became more than a geographical location; it evolved into a crucible of resilience and a canvas painted with hues of adversity.

The challenges, though daunting, were not mere stumbling blocks but threads that wove the fabric of my character. The shadows of familial struggles and the complexities of life in the projects molded me into a protagonist of my own narrative.

The asymmetry within our family dynamics, coupled with the strains of life in Dutch Quarter, thrust upon me a mantle of responsibility that belied my years.

The streets, once an escape, metamorphosed into a terrain where survival demanded not just courage but an ability to navigate the intricate dance of life. From the allure of quick money to the semblance of control it offered, the streets became both mentor and adversary, shaping my identity in ways unforeseen.

As I revisit these chapters of my life, I do so not with resentment but with an acknowledgment that every twist and turn was a brushstroke in the painting of my resilience.

The adversity, though heavy, propelled me forward, crafting a narrative that defies the conventional constraints of youth. Dutch Quarter, with its complexities and challenges, became the backdrop against which the journey of self-discovery unfolded.

Struggles My Family Went Through: Unveiling the Turbulence

The aftermath of the hurricane ushered in a period of immense upheaval for my family. In Dutch Quarter, a new chapter unfolded, but it was fraught with challenges and marked by the absence of my father.

In his place stepped my stepfather, introducing a new layer of complexity to our family dynamics. With my second brother and the arrival of twins, our 2-bedroom house became a crowded haven for four siblings, my mother, and stepfather. This was not the ideal setting for stability, and finding a foothold became a daily battle.

The economic landscape posed hurdles for my mother, who was accustomed to employment in the hotel sector. The income she could generate proved insufficient for a family of our size. Meanwhile, my stepfather, hailing from Anguilla, grappled with the constraints of lacking proper working documentation. His options were confined to sporadic, low-paying odd jobs, unable to provide the financial stability our family direly needed.

Within the confines of our home, a tumultuous atmosphere took root. My stepfather's penchant for returning home intoxicated only amplified the existing struggles.

The tranquility we sought remained elusive, overshadowed by daily arguments that seemed to erupt without any discernible cause.

As the oldest sibling, I sought refuge outside, away from the chaos that permeated our home. The streets became my sanctuary, and I immersed myself in the world beyond our front door, finding solace amidst the unpredictable challenges life presented.

Dynamics Within the Family: Navigating Unequal Waters

The introduction of my stepfather into our family unit brought with it a unique set of challenges. As he grappled with the complexities of a blended family, the distinctions between his biological children and my second brother and me became palpable.

These disparities extended beyond emotional nuances to affect basic necessities like food, access to the radio, and control over the TV.

Within this unequal landscape, my mother, confronted with the arduous task of ensuring fairness, resorted to hiding food for my second brother and me.

However, these covert attempts were often foiled, as my stepfather would unearth the hidden provisions, either consuming them himself or redirecting them to his biological children.

This dynamic thrust upon me the unexpected role of providing for myself and my younger brother, pushing me into a premature embrace of responsibility.

The strains within our family were not only financial but also emotional. The unequal treatment and the palpable tension at home propelled me into a realm of self-reliance that transcended the conventional boundaries of adolescence.

Faced with limited resources and a fractured family dynamic, I embarked on a journey of survival, navigating the intricate dance of Dutch Quarter life.

This journey became a catalyst for the development of my own resourcefulness, propelling me into a world that necessitated unconventional means for sustenance.

Life in Dutch Quarter: Navigating Turbulence

Life in Dutch Quarter, in the wake of the hurricane, became a battleground where the echoes of familial discord reverberated.

The challenges of our cramped living conditions, exacerbated by financial constraints, instilled in me a determination to navigate the turbulent waters of adolescence with resilience and adaptability.

The chaos within our home, characterized by my stepfather's erratic behavior, prompted me to seek solace outside its confines.

After the school bell rang, my siblings and I would linger outdoors, extending our stay until the return of my mother or stepfather. This external refuge became an essential coping mechanism, offering respite from the daily tumult within the walls of our home.

Despite the adversities, the spirit of survival thrived within me. The intricate dance of life in Dutch Quarter necessitated unconventional strategies for sustenance.

From packing bags to engaging in petty crimes, I found myself compelled to partake in a range of activities to secure a foothold in a world where stability seemed elusive.

The challenges of family life became intertwined with the complexities of the environment, forging a path that required not only resilience but an ability to adapt to the ever-shifting dynamics of Dutch Quarter.

The Resilience of Youth: Crafting a Path Forward

Amidst the shadows of familial struggles and the complexities of life in Dutch Quarter, the resilience of youth emerged as a guiding force. The struggles, though daunting, became the crucible in which my character was forged.

The disparities within our family, the financial limitations, and the tumultuous atmosphere at home were the threads that wove a narrative of survival.

As the oldest sibling, thrust into a position of unexpected responsibility, I navigated the challenges with a determination born out of necessity.

The streets of Dutch Quarter, despite their challenges, became a canvas on which I painted my journey-a journey that required resourcefulness, adaptability, and an unyielding spirit.

These formative years were not merely a sequence of adversities but a transformative period that laid the foundation for the person I would become.

The resilience cultivated amidst the struggles, the lessons learned in the crucible of familial discord, and the adaptability honed on the streets of Dutch Quarter shaped the contours of my character.

As I share these glimpses into the struggles my family endured, I do so not with bitterness but with an understanding that every challenge was a stepping stone, every adversity a lesson.

The turbulence of those years, though arduous, propelled me forward, instilling in me a resilience that would prove invaluable in the years to come.

The Incarceration Experience

The journey into the prison system began with the tumultuous backdrop of a dangerous neighborhood and a life of crime.

Fleeing the country due to escalating issues, Alesco faced unexpected challenges, including being separated from a loved one and discovering the betrayal of close friends who left without him.

Arrested on his mother's birthday, Alesco found himself in a cold room at the police station for about 90 days, enduring harsh conditions and questioning.

The daily routine was bleak, with inadequate facilities, rusty water, and deplorable living conditions. The atmosphere in the police station, coupled with the uncertainty of court proceedings, added a layer of despair to the challenges faced in Dutch Quarter.

Upon entering the prison system on January 11, 2011, Alesco was met with the reality of Point Blanche prison. The segregation based on gangs and neighborhoods was immediately apparent, and the guards, aware of Alesco's origin, placed him in a section with familiar faces from Dutch Quarter.

However, the initial sense of safety was overshadowed by the ominous chants of "fresh meat."

Life within the prison walls came with its own set of rules. No snitching and protecting one's "bling" were paramount.

The bling served as a lifeline to the outside world, a connection that had to be safeguarded at all costs. Earning respect and status within the prison community involved navigating a complex social hierarchy, a challenge Alesco willingly embraced.

In the face of adversity, Alesco chose not to succumb to the harsh environment but sought ways to better himself.

Encouraged to attend school by an older inmate, Alesco reluctantly participated in various classes, gaining skills and certificates. The routine included classes in computer skills, carpentry, welding, mechanics, cooking, sewing, and more.

The living conditions within the prison mirrored the brutality of the police station, with overcrowded cells, rusty bars, and unsanitary bathrooms.

Despite the hardships, Alesco found solace in activities like joining the church band and learning to play the bass guitar. Over the years, he encountered challenges, engaged in a few fights, and witnessed a tragic death within the prison walls.

As the journey continued, Alesco's perspective on life shifted. A profound realization dawned on him after witnessing a high-profile inmate being shot behind bars - the understanding that no one is untouchable.

Life in prison became a transformative journey, where survival required not just physical strength, but also resilience, adaptability, and a commitment to personal growth.

In the midst of adversity, Alesco found a way to navigate the complexities of prison life, ultimately emerging with a changed perspective on the fragility of life and the importance of resilience and self-improvement.
As Alesco delved deeper into prison life, he discovered the intricacies of survival. The unspoken code among inmates involved maintaining alliances, avoiding conflicts, and

navigating the delicate balance between respect and vulnerability.
Despite the challenges, Alesco continued to engage in activities that would contribute positively to his prison experience.

Joining the church band provided not only a creative outlet but also a sense of community within the prison walls. Learning to play the bass guitar became a form of therapy, allowing him to channel his emotions and find solace in the midst of confinement. The prison's routine, once monotonous and harsh, now had pockets of purpose and fulfillment.

Participation in various skill-building classes became a cornerstone of Alesco's rehabilitation. The certificates earned through these courses not only brought a sense of accomplishment but also offered opportunities for earning a modest income within the prison.

The importance of education and personal development became apparent as he gradually embraced a path of self-improvement.

While Alesco faced the daily challenges of prison life, the external world continued to evolve. The shifts in technology, politics, and society outside the prison walls were distant echoes, but Alesco remained connected to the unfolding events through sporadic communication with family and limited access to news.

Throughout the years, Alesco's resilience was put to the test. Facing fights and witnessing the tragic death of a fellow inmate forced him to confront the harsh realities of prison violence.

However, these experiences also fueled a determination to survive, adapt, and emerge stronger from the crucible of incarceration.

In the realm of prison dynamics, Alesco built a reputation not through violence but by staying true to his principles.

As he earned the respect of fellow inmates through genuine interactions and a commitment to personal growth, the prison environment slowly transformed. It became a space where shared struggles forged unlikely bonds, and the journey towards redemption took unexpected tums.

The story within the prison system became a narrative of resilience, transformation, and an exploration of the human spirit's capacity to evolve even in the harshest conditions. Alesco, once a product of a challenging environment in Dutch Quarter, began to redefine himself within the confined boundaries of Point Blanche prison.

The journey continued, with each passing day offering a chance for growth, reflection, and the possibility of a different future beyond the prison walls.

As Alesco continued to navigate the complex social fabric of the prison, he found himself drawn into unforeseen conflicts and alliances. The dynamics among inmates often mirrored the external world's complexities, with power struggles, unwritten hierarchies, and the constant ebb and flow of friendships and rivalries

Alesco's commitment to education and skill development became a source of inspiration for some inmates, while others viewed it with skepticism.
As he engaged in activities like carpentry, welding, and cooking, he became a symbol of resilience and determination. The journey within the prison system wasn't just about survival but also about leaving a lasting impact on those around him.

Alesco's interactions with the prison guards, initially marked by suspicion and authority, evolved over time. While maintaining a healthy distance, he learned to navigate the system, understanding that cooperation could sometimes ease the challenges of daily life behind bars.

The delicate dance between authority and autonomy became a constant theme in his prison experience.

Despite the confined space, the prison environment had its microcosm of cultural diversity. Inmates from different backgrounds, ethnicities, and walks of life coexisted within the prison walls.

This diversity brought both challenges and opportunities for understanding, tolerance, and sometimes unexpected friendships.

Over the years, Alesco became a witness to the ephemerality of human connections within the prison. Inmates came and went, each leaving an indelible mark on Alesco's journey. Some became trusted allies, while others were fleeting acquaintances, a reminder of the transient nature of relationships within the confines of Point Blanche prison.

Alesco's experience also unfolded against the backdrop of evolving prison policies and societal changes. Shifts in legislation, occasional visits from family members, and the intermittent influx of new inmates introduced an element of unpredictability to his routine.

Each adjustment required a recalibration of expectations and strategies for coping with the ever-changing prison landscape.

As the years passed, Alesco found himself grappling not only with the physical challenges of incarceration but also with the psychological toll it took. The monotony of prison life, the separation from loved ones, and the constant struggle for autonomy weighed heavily on his spirit.

Yet, within this struggle, he discovered pockets of resilience, moments of joy, and a profound capacity for self- discovery.

The journey within the prison system, initially marked by survival instincts, transformed into a saga of personal evolution.
Alesco's commitment to education, his engagement in positive activities, and his ability to forge meaningful connections within the prison community showcased the human spirit's innate capacity for growth, even in the most constrained circumstances.

The prison experience, a crucible of challenges and opportunities, became a canvas on which Alesco painted a narrative of resilience, redemption, and the unwavering pursuit of a better self. The story continued, each day offering new insights, unexpected twists, and the possibility of a brighter future beyond the prison walls.

Personal Growth and Reflection

During my time in prison, one key moment that deeply impacted my mindset and perspective on life was witnessing a violent incident within the prison walls.
While I didn't physically witness the act, being present in the prison while it took place served as a harsh reality check. It

made me realize that no one is untouchable, regardless of their status or background.

The incident emphasized the stark truth that, within those walls, anyone with enough influence and resources could make Someone disappear. It was a chilling realization that stayed with me throughout my incarceration.

Another significant aspect of my personal growth unfolded over the years as I observed my own transformation within the prison environment. Initially entering the system as a young and reckless individual, I gradually developed a sense of consciousness about my reality. I recognized the need to make the best of my living situation and adapt to the harsh environment surrounding me.

The absence of family and friends on the outside compelled me to rely on self-dependency and the skills I acquired over time to survive among murderers, rapists, and drug dealers.

Engaging in various activities, such as attending school and acquiring new skills, played a crucial role in shaping my sense of purpose and identity within the prison walls. These activities not only garnered respect from fellow inmates but also from the guards.

I built a reputation that allowed me to move more freely within the prison, and some guards even sought my assistance in improving communication and information exchange among them. This experience highlighted the importance of effective communication in life, a lesson I carried with me beyond the prison walls.

One notable activity that impacted my time behind bars was learning to play the bass guitar. It not only provided a form of self-expression but also allowed me to connect with like-minded individuals within the prison community.

Joining a group of individuals with a shared interest in playing instruments, particularly within a church setting, created a sense of camaraderie that further contributed to my personal growth.

Reflecting on the challenges I faced, the lessons I learned, and the experiences! encountered within the prison environment, I can attest that they collectively shaped my character. The harsh realities of limited resources and the constant threat of violence taught me resilience, adaptability, and the importance of staying focused on personal growth even in adverse conditions.

While the future seemed uncertain during my time in prison, with each passing day feeling like an eternity, I held onto the belief that anything that starts must have an ending.

This mindset propelled me forward, encouraging continuous progress and learning. I emerged from the prison system with a transformed outlook on life, grounded in the lessons learned and the personal growth achieved against all odds.

As my journey within the prison continued, I faced both internal and externa. challenges that further molded my character and outlook on life. One of the most Profound realizations came from the relationships I formed with fellow inmates.
Living among murderers, rapists, and drug dealers forced me to confront the resilience that challenged my preconceptions.
complexities of human nature. I witnessed stories of remorse, redemption, and
In the face of adversity, I found solace and support in unexpected places. The bonds

formed within the church community became a source of strength. It was within these walls that I discovered the power of faith, compassion, and the ability to find common ground despite diverse backgrounds.

The church provided not only a sanctuary for spiritual growth but also a platform for positive change and personal connection.

The challenges of limited resources within the prison environment pushed me to think creatively and find unconventional solutions. Whether it was sharing knowledge with fellow inmates, negotiating with guards for better conditions, or finding innovative ways to make the most of the available resources, every hurdle became an opportunity for growth. These experiences taught me the value of resourcefulness and the ability to navigate through adversity with resilience.

As the years passed, I found myself not only surviving but thriving in an environment that seemed designed to break individuals. The constant progression, learning, and self-improvement became a testament to the human spirit's capacity to endure and evolve, even in the harshest of conditions.

Looking back, I realized that my perspective on the future had transformed. Instead of viewing each day as an eternity, I embraced the idea that every moment, no matter how challenging, brought me closer to the eventual end of my sentence. This shift in mindset allowed me to set goals within the constraints of prison life, fostering a sense of purpose and direction.

The lessons learned within those prison walls went beyond the confines of physical space. I discovered the importance of empathy, resilience, and the capacity for personal growth in the face of adversity.

Emerging from that chapter of my life, I carried with me a newfound appreciation for the interconnectedness of humanity and the ability to find hope and meaning even in the most unlikely of places.

As my time in prison unfolded, I delved even deeper into the realms of self-discovery and personal development.

The library, although limited, became my haven, offering a gateway to knowledge and intellectual growth. I immersed myself in literature, philosophy, and various educational materials, expanding my understanding of the world beyond the prison walls.

This intellectual journey not only stimulated my mind but also gave me a broader perspective on life, challenging the boundaries of my own preconceived notions.

One of the pivotal moments in my transformation occurred during a mentorship program within the prison. I became a mentor to fellow inmates, guiding them through the challenges of prison life and imparting the lessons I had learned along the way.

This role not only solidified my own understanding of the lessons but also allowed me to witness the transformative power of mentorship in the lives of others. It was a profound realization of the positive impact one individual could have on another, even within the confines of a seemingly bleak environment.

The resilience and determination required to navigate prison life translated into a newfound sense of discipline. Establishing daily routines and setting personal goals became the pillars of my existence.

From physical fitness regimens to educational milestones, each accomplishment became a testament to the strength of the human spirit and the ability to thrive, regardless of the circumstances.

Moreover, the dynamics of social interaction within the prison community provided valuable insights into human behavior, fostering a deepened understanding of empathy and compassion.
Witnessing the stories of fellow inmates, their struggles, and triumphs, instilled in me a profound sense of empathy for the human condition.
These connections, forged in adversity, emphasized the shared humanity that transcends societal labels and judgments.

As my release date approached, the prospect of reintegration into society loomed large. The anticipation of freedom was met with a mix of excitement and apprehension. The prison environment had become a cocoon of growth and self-discovery, and stepping beyond its walls meant facing a world vastly different from the one I had known before incarceration.

In retrospect, my time in prison became a transformative journey, marked by resilience, learning, and an unyielding commitment to personal growth. It was a testament to the indomitable human spirit's capacity to evolve, adapt, and find purpose even in the most challenging circumstances.

As I prepared to leave the prison behind, I carried with me a wealth of experiences, lessons, and a profound sense of gratitude for the opportunity to redefine my life beyond the confines of the past.

Relationships in Prison: Forming bonds

During my time in prison spanning 11 years and 4 months, I forged numerous relationships with both inmates and guards. I discovered that everyone has a story, and many would open up to me without prompting.

While I never intended to play the role of a lawyer, I became a listener, understanding that some individuals just needed someone to hear their tales. The prison environment, with its diverse community, posed challenges and opportunities for forming bonds and navigating friendships.

In building relationships with inmates, I learned to be selective, realizing that forming bonds with those serving significantly shorter sentences might result in them leaving me behind.

Given my own lengthy 19-year sentence, I chose to associate with individuals serving similar terms. One notable connection was with a man from Dominica, whom I lived with for six consecutive years. Despite occasional arguments, our bond resembled that of father and son.

Living with foreign inmates taught me resilience, adaptability, and the ability to survive. Hurricane Irma forced me to relocate to Curaçao temporarily, where I formed bonds with others facing similar challenges. These connections, like the one with a Dominican named "Belly," endured even after our release, evolving into a sense of brotherhood

Continuing with my experiences in prison, the bonds formed in the church community went beyond music. Reverend Myrna Lake, in her role as a spiritual guide, not only led us in prayer but also instilled a sense of discipline and purpose. Despite her health struggles, she remained committed to our spiritual growth, leaving an indelible mark on my prison journey.

The church band not only allowed me to showcase my musical talents but also exposed me to the realities of the outside world.
As we played in different churches, I observed the development of the country and witnessed the passage of time through the growth of families. Meeting people who had supported us during our incarceration and seeing them share their joys and sorrows with us created a profound connection.

Being part of the church community granted me a unique perspective on the transformative power of faith. It provided solace, encouragement, and a sense of belonging. The church became a sanctuary within the prison walls, a place where we could momentarily escape the harsh reality of confinement and find spiritual nourishment.

Throughout this journey, I also encountered challenges and conflicts within the prison environment. However, the relationships I had cultivated, both with inmates and guards, served as pillars of support. These connections not only shaped my daily life but also influenced my growth as an individual.

The mutual respect established with guards allowed for a level of freedom and trust that transcended the typical inmate-guard dynamic.

As the years passed, my mindset evolved. I started mentoring younger inmates, emphasizing the importance of respect, resilience, and utilizing the available resources for personal development. My experiences became lessons, and the relationships formed served as conduits for positive change within the prison community.

In the latter years of my sentence, I began participating in educational programs offered within the prison. These initiatives not only broadened my knowledge but also provided a platform to share insights with fellow inmates. It became evident that education and personal growth were essential elements for rehabilitation and reintegration into society.

Ultimately, my release marked the culmination of over a decade spent behind bars.
The relationships forged during my time in prison, be it with inmates, guards, or the church community, played a pivotal role in shaping my perspective on life. The bonds formed endured beyond the prison walls,

leaving a lasting impact on my sense of purpose, well-being, and the person I had become. The lessons learned within those confined spaces became the foundation for a new chapter of my life outside the prison system.

In the realm of prison guards, I recognized the importance of respect. Many guards and I had known each other from before they assumed their roles, having attended school together on the small island of Saint Martin. I developed trust and respect with some guards, allowing for open conversations within limits. As a result, I gained a certain level of freedom within the prison, and some guards even left their positions when I was released, as they had promised.

The church community played a significant role in my prison experience, offering connections that contributed to my sense of purpose and well-being. I made friends

within the church, forming a band to fill the void left by departed musicians.
Reverend Myrna Lake became a mother figure, guiding us spiritually. Despite her illness, she held on until we completed our last performance outside the prison walls.
The church band provided opportunities to leave the prison periodically, showcasing our musical talents to different congregations.
This experience allowed me to witness the changes in the outside world and reconnect with people who had visited us during our incarceration.

The church became a source of freedom, personal development, and lasting connections that persisted even after my release.

Transition and New Beginnings

Returning to Dutch Quarter was like stepping into a world that had moved on without me. The familiar streets, once distant memories, now unfolded before me. However, the disconnect between the life I left behind and the one I was returning to was palpable.

As I walked through the neighborhood, I couldn't help but notice the changes - new faces, renovated buildings, and an evolving landscape. The reintegration process had already begun, and I was an observer navigating through the complexities of the world I once knew.

The ankle monitor strapped to my leg served as a constant reminder of the limitations that still bound me. House arrest became both a form of liberation and confinement - a paradox that mirrored the conflicting emotions swirling within me. Reconnecting with family and friends, who had been distant voices during my time away, became both a source of comfort and a challenge. Relationships strained by time and circumstances needed mending, and trust had to be rebuilt one interaction at a time.

Seeking employment in a society that often stigmatizes ex-convicts proved to be a daunting task. The weight of my criminal record loomed over every job application, casting shadows on my aspirations. The resilience forged within prison walls fueled my determination to overcome these obstacles.

I turned towards the skills I honed in the prison kitchen, seeking opportunities in the culinary world. Despite the rejections and skeptical glances, I persisted, driven by the desire to redefine my identity beyond the confines of a criminal label.

The process of securing employment, mending relationships, and adapting to a fast-paced society brought forth a wave of emotions. The struggle between the urge to conform and the determination to remain true to myself became a daily battle. The yearning for a sense of belonging, for acceptance, echoed within me as I navigated the challenges of reintegrating into a society that had moved forward without me.

In the midst of this struggle, music emerged as a familiar companion. While the chapel performances in Point Blanche were distant memories, the rhythm of the guitar strings and the melody of familiar tunes provided solace.

I sought opportunities to reignite my passion for music, connecting with local musicians and exploring avenues to share my talents. The guitar that survived Hurricane Irma became a symbol of resilience, a reminder that even in the face of destruction, some things endure.

As days turned into weeks and weeks into months, the monotony of house arrest gave way to a gradual sense of freedom. The ankle monitor, once a symbol of restriction, became a tool for accountability. It forced me to confront the consequences of my actions and make conscious choices about the path I wished to tread.
The support of a few understanding individuals in the community played a crucial role in my journey, offering guidance and encouragement during moments of doubt.

The day the ankle monitor was finally removed marked a symbolic moment of liberation. The weight lifted, and a newfound sense of freedom accompanied me as 1 stepped into a world that held both challenges and possibilities.

The experiences within the prison system, the trials of Hurricane Irma, and the hurdles of reintegration had sculpted a version of myself that was resilient, determined, and yearning for a second chance.

The journey didn't end with the removal of the ankle monitor. Instead, it marked the beginning of a new chapter - one where the scars of the past served as reminders of strength rather than weaknesses. Embracing the lessons learned, I forged ahead, seeking to break the cycle that had kept me entangled in the criminal justice system for far too long

In the quest for redemption, I became an advocate for prison reform, sharing my story to shed light on the struggles faced by those attempting to reintegrate into society. The experiences of Hurricane Irma and the challenges of adapting to foreign prison systems became narratives that fueled my commitment to contribute positively to the community.

As I ventured into entrepreneurship, starting small businesses and contributing to local initiatives, I aimed not only to rebuild my life but also to make a meaningful impact on the lives of others.

The journey from Point Blanche to the bustling streets of Dutch Quarter wasn't just a physical transition; it was a testament to the resilience of the human spirit and the capacity for change and growth.

The story of survival, adaptation, and reintegration became a living testament to the belief that transformation is possible, even in the face of the harshest storms.

The scars of the past became stories of triumph, and the future held the promise of a life redefined, shaped not by the prison bars but by the choices made beyond them.

With the ankle monitor removed and a renewed sense of purpose, I delved deeper int my commitment to community service. As an advocate for prison reform, I sought opportunities to share my experiences with local schools and community centers, hoping to inspire change and challenge the stereotypes associated with ex-convicts.
The challenges I faced during reintegration became fuel for my passion to create a more compassionate and understanding society.

Drawing from the resilience cultivated in prison, I initiated workshops aimed at providing essential life skills to those navigating the delicate transition from incarceration to freedom.
Topics ranged from job readiness to emotional well-being, each session rooted in the belief that empowering individuals with

the right tools could pave the way for a smoother reintegration process.

Simultaneously, my entrepreneurial spirit led me to create opportunities for others facing similar challenges. I collaborated with local organizations to establish small businesses that prioritized hiring individuals with criminal records, offering a chance for redemption and a fresh start. The process of rebuilding wasn't only about personal transformation; it extended to uplifting the broader community.
The scars of Hurricane Irma, both physical and emotional, fueled my commitment to environmental causes. I became involved in local initiatives focused on rebuilding and fortifying communities against future natural disasters.

The lessons learned during those tumultuous days inside the prison walls became a driving force for resilience, not just for myself but for the entire community.

Music, a constant companion throughout my journey, took on a new role as a tool for healing and empowerment. I collaborated with local musicians to organize music therapy sessions within correctional facilities, recognizing the profound impact that creative expression could have on the well-being of inmates. The chapel performances that once defined my purpose inside prison walls transformed into a means of fostering hope and inspiration for those still serving their sentences.

As my story gained visibility, I found support from unexpected quarters.

Local leaders, recognizing the potential for positive change, extended opportunities for collaboration and mentorship. Together, we worked towards dismantling the systemic barriers that hindered the reintegration process, advocating for policies that prioritized rehabilitation over punishment.

The journey from Point Blanche to community leader was marked by setbacks, triumphs, and continuous self-discovery.

Challenges persisted, but each obstacle became a stepping stone towards personal and societal transformation. The narrative of my life became intertwined with a broader narrative - one of resilience, redemption, and the collective pursuit of a more compassionate society.

The scars of the past, whether inflicted by the hurricane or the prison experience, became symbols of strength rather than sources of shame.

The journey continued to unfold, marked by a commitment to break the cycle of incarceration and contribute to the betterment of the community that had witnessed my struggles and triumphs.

In the realm of personal relationships, trust was a delicate thread that required careful weaving. Rebuilding connections with family and friends demanded time, patience, and a willingness to confront the complexities of fractured bonds.

As the months passed, the bonds strengthened, and the understanding deepened, fostering an environment of support that played a pivotal role in my ongoing journey.

Looking back on the arduous path, I realized that the story of reintegration was not a linear trajectory but a mosaic of experiences, challenges, and growth.

The narrative extended beyond my individual journey; it became a testament to the transformative power of resilience, compassion, and the collective will to forge a more inclusive and understanding society. As the pages of my life continued to turn, I embraced the uncertainty of the future with a newfound sense of optimism.

The journey from Point Blanche had not only reshaped my identity but also presented an opportunity to contribute meaningfully to the world beyond prison walls.

The road ahead was paved with potential, and the echoes of my story resonated not only within my own heart but within the community that had become an integral part of my redemption narrative.

To the young souls currently entangled in the web of crime

The Power of Redemption

In the crucible of life, where every action leaves an indelible mark, the power of redemption stands as a testament to the resilience of the human spirit.

As I reflect on the shadows of my past, I am reminded that redemption is not a mere concept; it is a living force that has the capacity to transform even the darkest chapters of our lives. It's an inner flame that flickers within every soul, waiting to be kindled and radiate warmth.

Despite the mistakes that led me to the unforgiving confines of prison, discovered that redemption is not an unattainable ideal; it is a path that beckons e one of us to rise from the ashes of our past selves.

The journey toward redemption is a labyrinthine exploration of self-discovery, forgiveness, and personal evolution. It demands introspection, an unflinching gaze into the mirror of one's own actions, and the courage to confront the shadows that linger within.

It is a pilgrimage that requires acknowledging not only the pain inflicted upon others but also the wounds we carry within ourselves.

Through the crucible of remorse and self-reflection, I found that the power of redemption lies not in erasing the past but in

transforming its echoes into stepping stones toward a better
future.

As the currents of redemption flowed through the river of my life, I realized that its power extended beyond the realm of personal salvation. It possesses the capacity to mend fractured relationships, to bridge chasms between hearts estranged by past wrongs.

It's an elixir that, when administered with sincerity, has the potential to heal wounds, rebuild trust, and resurrect bonds that seemed irreparably broken. The power of redemption is not a solitary force but a harmonizing melody that, when embraced, orchestrates a symphony of healing and renewal.

In the crucible of redemption, one discovers that forgiveness is not merely a gift bestowed upon others but a transformative act that liberates the soul. It is an offering to oneself, a liberation from the chains of guilt and self-condemnation.

Redemption, in its truest form, is a tapestry woven from the threads of forgiveness, resilience, and the unwavering belief in the human capacity to transcend its own limitations.

The Road to Transformation

The road to transformation is a formidable journey that demands a courageous exploration of the self— a pilgrimage from the shadows of the past into the illumination of self-discovery.

As I traversed this path, I encountered the echoes of my own mistakes, the weight of my transgressions pressing heavily upon my shoulders. Yet, it was within this crucible of self-awareness that I discovered the transformative potential residing in the recesses of my being.

Transformation is not a sudden metamorphosis but a gradual unfolding — a shedding of layers that no longer serve, and a rebirth into a truer, more authentic self. It requires a willingness to confront the vulnerabilities concealed beneath the armor of bravado, to delve into the depths of one's fears, and to emerge, cleansed and renewed, from the crucible of introspection.

The road to transformation is often challenging, but within its challenges lies the crucible of self-evolution.

The transformative journey extends beyond the individual, reaching into the reams of relationships and connections with others. It is a ripple effect — a profound alteration that not only reshapes the individual but also influences the dynamics of interpersonal bonds.

As I embraced the process of transformation, I witnessed the mending of fractured relationships, the restoration of trust, and the blossoming of connections that transcended the scars of the past. Transformation, at its core, is a harmonizing force that extends its influence far beyond the solitary seeker.
In the pursuit of transformation, resilience emerges as a stalwart companion. It is the unwavering resolve to persist in the face of adversity, the inner strength that enables one to navigate the turbulent waters of change. Resilience is not merely a survival instinct but a guiding light that illuminates

the path to self-discovery. It is the force that empowers individuals to confront their deepest fears, overcome challenges, and emerge on the other side, transformed and reborn.

The Tapestry of Hope

Within the intricate tapestry of life, hope stands as the golden thread that weaves through the fabric of existence. It is the beacon that beckons individuals from the abyss of despair toward the shores of possibility.

As I reflect on my own journey, hope emerged as the catalyst for transformation—a radiant force that dispelled the shadows of doubt and illuminated the path toward a brighter future.

Hope is not a passive yearning but an active force that propels individuals forward, even in the face of seemingly insurmountable odds. It is the belief in the potential for change, the conviction that tomorrow holds the promise of renewal.

In the darkest corners of despair, hope becomes the light that guides the way, instilling the courage to persevere through the storm and navigate toward calmer shores.
The tapestry of hope extends beyond the individual, threading its luminous essence through the relationships and connections that define our lives.

It is a collective force that unites communities, mends the fabric of fractured societies, and fosters a shared vision for a better tomorrow.

As I embraced the transformative journey, hope became a bridge connecting hearts that had been estranged by the shadows of the past. It is a force that unifies, heals, and rejuvenates the communal spirit.

Hope is a testament to the resilience of the human spirit— an unwavering belief that, regardless of the past, the future is an open canvas waiting to be painted with the strokes of possibility.

It fuels the courage to confront the challenges that lie ahead, to transcend the limitations of circumstance, and to envision a destiny shaped by optimism and aspiration. In the grand tapestry of existence, hope is the golden thread that binds together the chapters of adversity, redemption, and transformation.

Closing Words of Heartfelt Encouragement

To the brave souls entangled in the intricate web of crime, I extend my heartfelt words as a testament to the power of redemption and the transformative journey that awaits.

As I inscribe these final reflections, it is not merely a story that unfolds before you but a real-life chronicle— an odyssey marked by the passage of time, the consequences of choices, and the enduring hope for change.

In the crucible of life, where every trial becomes a stepping stone toward transformation, remember that the power of redemption is not reserved for the distant realms of myth; it is a tangible force that resides within the core of your being.

Embrace the journey of self-discovery, confront the shadows of your past with courage, and recognize that every mistake carries the potential for growth and evolution.

The road to transformation may appear daunting, but within its twists and turns lies the promise of a rebirth —a shedding of the old self and the emergence of a truer, more resilient you.

As you navigate this path, cherish the bonds of connection with those who believe in your potential for change. Seek knowledge, acquire skills, and invest in your personal development, for the human spirit possesses an innate capacity for transcendence, even within the confines of adversity.

The tapestry of hope, woven from the threads of resilience and optimism, extends its luminous embrace toward you. In the midst of despair, remember that hope is not an illusion but a force capable of illuminating even the darkest corners of your existence.

Your potential is not confined to the limitations of crime; you possess the agency to shape a different legacy, one characterized by purpose, growth, and positive impact.

As I offer these words of encouragement, I do so with the deepest sincerity and the unwavering belief that change is not only possible but imminent. Life, despite its trials, is a tapestry waiting to be woven with the threads of redemption, resilience, and triumph.

Embrace the transformative journey with an open heart, for within the crucible of change, you may discover a version of yourself that transcends the shadows of the past.

To the young souls navigating the labyrinth of choices, may these words resonate within the recesses of your being, stirring a profound awakening to the boundless potential that lies within.

This is not just a story; this is the essence of real life-an exploration of the human spirit's capacity for redemption, transformation, and the enduring pursuit of a brighter tomorrow.

With sincere conviction,
Alesco E. Violenes

One who has walked the treacherous path and found a way back to the light.

A note to myself........

Thank You Notes

I extend my heartfelt gratitude to the friends who provided valuable insights since embarking on this journey: Joel Pantol, Dolton Leblanc, Isidro Peterson, and Chef Giovanni Jermain. I am deeply grateful for your guidance.

A special thank you goes to Myrna Lake. Your spiritual mentorship and unwavering support during my darkest days illuminated a path forward. It means the world to me.

I am indebted to the individuals in my resource circle; your advice is truly appreciated.

I would like to express my heartfelt gratitude to my book purchasers and readers. Thank you for your interest, time, support, and investment in my story.

I hope that by sharing these difficult truths, I might help others find their way without having to walk a similar path.

The Story Behind This Book

I never thought about writing a book while in prison. As my release date drew closer, another inmate asked me, "What will you do when you get out of here?"

"Boy, I don't know," I replied honestly.

"Well, you should write a book about your time in this place," he suggested. "Your story needs to be told."

That brief conversation planted a seed in my mind that refused to die. In the quiet hours of my cell, I began to consider what such a book might contain—not just the hardships of imprisonment, but the complete journey that brought me there and the transformation that occurred behind those walls.

After my release, that seed continued to grow. I started jotting down memories, piecing together the fragments of my past, and reflecting on how Point Blanche had changed me.

What began as casual writing sessions evolved into a purposeful project as I realized how many young people might benefit from hearing my story.

Now, years later, that casual suggestion has blossomed into the book you hold in your hands—the harvest of a seed planted during one ordinary conversation in an extraordinary place.

I hope that through sharing my journey, others might find their own path to transformation without having to first lose their freedom......

Surviving Point Blanche Prison

Made in the USA
Columbia, SC
25 May 2025

58301017R00043